SLEEPLESS

Julia Deakin was born in Nuneaton and meandered north via the Potteries, Manchester and York, to Huddersfield where she taught, married, did a poetry MA and took up ice skating. Her collections include *The Half-Mile-High Club* (a 2007 Poetry Business Competition winner), *Without a Dog* (Graft, 2008) and *Eleven Wonders* (Graft, 2012). She has featured twice on *Poetry Please* and won numerous prizes – none of them for skating.

Sleepless

JULIA DEAKIN

Valley Press

First published in 2018 by Valley Press
Woodend, The Crescent, Scarborough, YO11 2PW
www.valleypressuk.com

First edition, first printing (September 2018)

ISBN 978-1-912436-10-1
Cat. no. VP0130

A CIP record for this book is available from the British Library.

Cover illustration: 'Hope' by George Frederic Watts and assistants, 1886.
Cover and text design by Jamie McGarry.
Edited by Char March.

Printed and bound in the EU by Pulsio, Paris.

Contents

CLOZE PROCEDURE

SLEEPLESS

Just as a train

arriving next to yours
can make you think you're moving off at last
towards the next stage of your life

and snow, entailed in wind or rain,
can fall so stealthily at first you blink,
unsure if it is falling

or you are rising –
you, the room you're in
and all the lights and tables floating

up from the soiled earth
through gassy layers to moon-pastures,
planets, galaxies –

so love, new as the marble hills
may fall to you.

The knowledge

for John Duffy

The birds have paths they follow through the air
as urgently as city strap-hangers, each arc
from nest to bough to open ground determined
by the day's light rations and the hour's need –
to build, to mate, to roost, to outdo predators.
By hedges, fences, fields and lanes then up
on thermal elevators over rooftops along valleys
towards estuaries, one wing-tip angled to the sun
they surge along magnetic corridors
as unmarked and beyond our fenced imaginings
as when the earth's first migrant wings
beat down horizons ridge by ridge, sea after sea
in search of fresh springs, kinder hemispheres.

Only a goldfish

is equipped to see the full colour spectrum,
from infra-red to ultra-violet – the rush
when we open our crude human eyes
under water as nothing to this lysergic trip.

Nor, without eyelids, can they shut off
the circus, but must party on nightly
ten or more years – lifelong sleep deprivation
enough to fry any brain. And theirs is big:

from a line-up they might well distinguish
their owners' rainbow hair, clothes and auras
from those of the Christmas holiday minder
or the man who fixed the boiler.

Come March with a three-month memory span
they'd still know who was where on the night
in question. And might tell you if they talked.

Which, as they nose round forever on the case,
they doubtless do.

Search & Rescue

Just after we'd been learning how to sing
by breathing from the diaphragm, we heard.
Felt the engines slow then circle all day
underneath the cold sun, moving and yet still –
the ship making loops within its course
as we made smaller circuits of the deck.

Silent, thinking we might hear cries, we leaned
on rails, conscious of our breath, stared out
and down, turned binoculars, sifted fact
from speculation as the sea flexed its blue muscle,
shifted glaucous eyes. When they found her
face down, floating 'like a plastic bag',
we thought of lungs – the act, the art of breathing.

Lost

Germany's beyond me now, the bits I gleaned
at school from a Jewish teacher for a GCE
(itself history) *ganz vergessen.* The words –
niemals, Regenbogen, Brustwarze – rankled
for not being French. Dative, ablative, accusative:
even the English words about it baffled.

My parents thought it mattered more than Spanish
and once, looking for a youth hostel near Bonn,
made me speak some. *Wohin Venusberg?*
I ventured, from the back of the Hillman Hunter
over Mum. The reply losing us, we argued
for the next half hour until we got there. Sometimes
scraps float back, sly as calculus or gene theory.
Arbeit. Vergissmeinnicht. Starnbergersee.

Sleepless

think of lakes. Lakes you have known
and great ones, the size of countries, known
only of. Of how you can – if you can – know

a body of water. Waters you've skirted
as they kept pace and held their peace.
Those whose hems you have touched.

Under the same more silent dark, find
all the lakes of the nightside hemisphere –
reach beneath their skin. The Cumbrians

flooring the fells – prone but restless,
acres and acres of eyes, outstaring
the livelong night, reflecting nothing in parts

but moonless sky, drowning the negligible stars;
then all the lochs and lochans of Scotland
in the colder dark, under the same sky

ticking, lapping, breathing, systole/diastole:
dive   to take that wild arhythmic pulse,
taste that deep indifference.

Landlocked

Black, brown and green from east to west
the only glimmers here are roofs,
the only rivers, roads.

Adrift, we scan horizons
until clouds torn briefly under sun
reveal, far off but twinkling,
a lake –

which once found is found again more easily
until, straining a lens beyond the possible towards the microscopic
fleck on fleck, speck on sparkle there appears
a boat.

Red kite over Harehills Lane

When the kite builds, look to lesser linen.
The Winter's Tale

Ten seconds at the lights present a sight
unseen in Leeds since Shakespeare's day,
when these 'har' hills were bare and grey,
Oakwood just an oak wood. Stranger,
welcome back from your diaspora.

As gulls tow fishing ports inland, this hawk
brings open vistas, promontories, visions
of a world elsewhere. Above the vying signs –
Electrotown, Your Loan Shop,
Lota Properties – she soars
off kilter like a toy kite in the diesel fret,
pinpointing a washing line, a risky rat,
two skips behind the Polski Sklep.

From this fraught junction of the disparate,
pluck hope: that the improbable is possible.
Tonight she'll tuck a Hello Kitty glove
into the twigs to signal 'nest on song'.
Tides turn. Hearts change. It need not take so long.

Armley Clock School

Now it's a business centre, cheaper than downtown Leeds,
where private healthcare clients get fast-track diagnoses
and young guns parking under the clock tower's symmetry
don't see asylums, workhouses or transit termini
but 'an impressive building, redeveloped to provide
modern office suites within gated landscaped grounds'.

Few still left remember their playground's past: the feathers
of pale blue candy-floss that floated over the Aviary's estate
from Roberts' asbestos works, to whiten the coke heap
and soot-black brick, tinsel the window cords and fall
like the warm dry snow of dreams, into the paradise kids make
of whatever they find. Game after game they played out
the best years of their lives, under the ticking clock.

Invisible

This is a passenger announcement: we are now
approaching Leeds. Look out to see the world-famous statue
gliding into view. Eleven storeys high from the door
in his heel, you can climb the staircase inside
to the windows in his ears, should you so wish.

Built in nineteen eighty-nine, this much-loved icon
stands for everyone who comes to work or study here
then stays and gives their all. As you know
the Brick Man – star of Instagram and Snapchat –
is the North's Big Ben, and made the sculptor's name.

Asked what he'd have done if Leeds had said no,
Gormley said some kind of metal angel.
Lucky Leeds acquired the tribute it deserved –
to long-termism: vision, art, and nerve.

Virgin territory

This is a Virgin Train:
a *Virgin Voyager*, no less.
(Does that explain the nets
behind the seats, crying out for
handfuls of fresh fish?)

I have an *airline-type seat,*
which means I find no window
but a piece of moulded off-white plastic,
the better maybe to imagine
flight through seas of cloud
from Manchester to New Street.

The seats have ears – red and blue –
like ranks of Mickey Mouses. Mickey Mice.

This Virgin train, Myfanwy tells me
on the tannoy, *has an area for retail sales –*
no shop, then – and *Stockport*
is our next station stop. There being,
evidently, other kinds of stop.

Along the carpet (blue,
with unnerving blood-red streaks) confetti
ticket-clippings in the shape of threes
evoke more soothing thoughts
of weddings, and the promise
that, Virgin though the train may be,
this seat is not reserved.

Ascending and descending

M.C. Escher, 1960

are you
the one   storey or story
at the front   sentry
with your back   then which century
to us or the one   is it then
facing white space   is it now
on the steps below   is it them
hidden from sight   is it us
of the cellars or cells   of a limbless cross
with the grilles   topped with the stump
at the foot of the   watchtower
palace or garrison   of a wedding-cake
warder or prisoner   through the eye
who is it you in   the courtyard to pace
the dark in the black   the square overlooking
that is doorless   captives who circle
who falls or   rations for captor or
is pushed through   like blisters of air or of
uncountable   rectangular domes
floors to   under rows of
a void

Proceed to checkout

What have we here, Walt Whitman? How you presume
on our millennial attention. We who have streams of memes
competing for it, so little time to listen, so many clamourers
for Likes, so many choices from so much clickbait thrust at us.

When you presumed in 1855, a century before my birth,
America teemed with entrepreneurs whose lessons, learned
a safe distance from the Old World, still gave them hope of a New
(a continent merely to prise from its peaceable peoples),

Leaves of Grass was a rationale against gods and demagogues.
I have the copy my grandmother treasured as the extant wisdom
of her elders. But oh You Grand Narratives! How you seduced.
You Overarching Theories! You Universal Truths!

You first, intemperate Gods, benign and vengeful antinomians
charging about the skies. You Fates writ large as stars.
You portents, comets, astral bodies, planetary alignments –
You zodiacal twelve houses, to which all types conformed.

You Mystics, Shamans, Stoics, Epicureans. You Numerologists.
You Pantheists. You Natural Philosophers. You Occultists.
You Doctors. You Economists. You Fundamentalists. You Ists.
You data-journals-papers-books no rational public can deny.

What drives then, sex or power? All we discover are more icons,
more iconoclasts, more plaques, more statues. That sense
of having found where all roads lead, what everything comes
    down to.
That meaning everyone desires: that everyone desires meaning.

You epiphany-junkies, surfing in on new waves of adherents,
colossi bestriding and colouring centuries, nations, ages.
How easy if there were one principle to which all things related
by which all were clarified, all loose ends tied;

if time and space were stable and consistent with infinity; if
The Ascent of Man had been a democratic song. Today, Walt,
we have painkillers: prophylactics wrapped in contra-indications.
Fake news. Relative values. Each of us innocent, till proven guilty.

Viareggio, 1822

That man Trelawney does nothing by halves:
the portable furnace he has rigged up
straddles the shingle like some cosmic craft,
or one of Shelley's own premonitions.

Byron! Hunt assails me: *you are too late...*
his flesh was completely gnawed... we knew him
only by his clothes – and by my copy of Keats,
folded back, I suppose, as he... I back off.

What can one ever say? Hard to believe
it's not another of his pranks – that our Ariel
might not creep up waggishly and whisper *atheist*
in my ear. Hard, too, over the stove's hiss

to recall his verse – while Keats, who drowned
in his own bed, still reverberates. Who knows
whose voice will carry them beyond
their native century – or even this next squall?

The Swan

Translated from Baudelaire's 'Le Cygne' (1857)

for Victor Hugo

Andromache, I think of you. That melancholy
meagre stream – once the resplendent mirror
of your widowhood's immense majesty –
that false Simoïs, swollen with your tears

came back to seed my fertile memory
as I traversed the brand new Carrousel.
Old Paris is no more (a city's shape, alas,
changes more quickly than the mortal heart.)

I still see in my mind the camp of huts,
the heaps of rough-hewn shafts and capitals,
the grass, the puddle-stained green blocks,
the jumbled lot reflected in the tiles.

Once a menagerie had covered it
where, one clear morning, in that hour
when under cold skies Work bestirs itself
and road sweepers storm the silent air – I saw

a swan, who had escaped his cage, dragging
his webbed feet along the dry pavement,
his white plumage trailing in the dirt.
By a parched ditch the bird opened his beak,

nervously flapped his wings there in the dust
and cried, heart bursting with his native lake,
'Water, when will you rain? Storm, when will you
roar?' I see this hapless creature, strange, doomed myth,

head straining to the sky like Ovid's man –
towards the blue sky's cruel irony –
his hungry head on his convulsive neck
as if addressing his complaint to God.

Paris changes, but my sombre mood
does not. New palaces, old suburbs, blocks
and scaffolding strike me as allegorical,
my memories heavier than rocks.

And so outside the Louvre one sight haunts:
of my great swan with his wild gestures
like all exiles, scorned and yet sublime,
gnawed by inconsolable desire. And of you too,

Andromache, from a great consort's arms
fallen to chatteldom at Pyrrhus' hands,
in passion bowed beside an empty tomb;
Hector's widow, Helenus's wife;

and of the thin, consumptive African,
gaunt eyes scanning as she trails through mud
for palm trees from her splendid continent
behind the massive barrier of fog;

and of those who lose what cannot ever –
ever – be retrieved. Who steep themselves
in tears and drink the she-wolf Sorrow's milk.
Of scrawny orphans shrivelling like flowers.

Here in the forest of my exiled soul
old memory's clarion call is loud and clear.
I think of castaways the world forgot,
of captives, the defeated and of more… so many more.

Screen saver

And you almost didn't bother
with that stone arch in the corner of the square
which only seemed to frame another wall your head still full
of Wells Cathedral's wavy steps and hidden octagons and saints
and bosses and misericords and ogives and the thought
of all those Jude the Obscures underpinning every church
you've ever sniffed around and the religious mummery and wars
and Larkin's Arundel and can you see a tomb without his glasses
looming mappa mundi cloistered monks and nuns and Dawkins'
God Delusion yes your mind's still full of all that dark dark dark

as you step through the archway

and the place you saw once in a dream is there that aisle
of silver stretching off beside a long sheer castellated wall
enclosing someone's secret garden trees above a single round door
only boats or swans can reach and two are nesting on a strip of grass
and six brown cygnets like big balls of wool watch families strolling
in the shade between the sycamores and lichened coping stones
receding towards meadows cows a wooded hill an idyll
your computer has fished up for you and now dissolves
into another: banks of purple heather
over Langsett Reservoir

In The Sanctuary of Mercy

Borja, Spain

They crowed, all those reporters – tore in
to my good work as if I was a criminal.
The priest disowned me, but I've made him rich –
packed in the crowds like his mass never did.

He just prayed – for the damp to stop, for cash,
a miracle – but we know who God helps.
Worn out, His face was – eighty years
stuck in a doorway takes it out of you.

Who knows what Our Lord looks like anyway?
Why not bad hair or shapeless clothes, if He
was poor like us? *Lovingly* I patched His coat
a warm brown from Brico King. That eye
took hours. The nose I'm quite proud of, too –
that's how Picasso does them. Had a few goes
at the mouth, but when you get inspired
where do you stop? He looks more – manly –
somehow. As if he might put up a fight.

Much thanks I got so yes, I'm suing –
and He's on my side, I reckon. Smiling, look.

Manners maketh

A muttered *thank god* and out of the blue
a deep voice in my ear's going *No, I insist –*
thank You. Without You I'd be nothing, nowhere.
You didn't always believe in me, but You made me
believe in myself. Here's a nice card signed by us all
and no Papermate pen but a whopping bouquet
no chrysanths and the rest of the whip-round
to spend as you please.

　　　　　　　　Some seraphim stomp and whoop,
one yells *Speech!* but the Boss bats on: *Not only me*
but everyone upstairs saw how You slogged away
all those years so thank You, thank You. And no
it's not time for your pearly gates yet: go and live
a bit longer more happily, with the karma
of One Who Has Been Thanked.
Thank You. I owe everything to You.

Last days

after Stanley Spencer

Blessed are the bolt-tighteners,
whose dances went unsung:
for they shall be serenaded.

Blessed are the dustmen
who bore the wasted world:
for they shall be carried like heroes.

Blessed are the teapots, the jam tins
and the cabbage stalks:
for they shall be made whole again.

Blessed is the furnace man,
who tended fire all his days:
for he shall himself be tended.

Blessed are the women
excluded from the bigger picture:
for they too shall be exalted.

Blessed are the naked,
who let ants crawl over them:
for they shall be robed and comforted.

Blessed are the riveters,
whose thunder made them deaf:
for they shall hear the music of leaves.

Blessed are the riggers,
whose fingers bled raw:
for they shall be held and anointed.

Blessed are the makers, good and bad:
for they shall climb from their graves
and not be judged.

'How can I tell if the bluebells in my garden are Spanish?'

They will be more flamboyant – their skirts flouncier,
more shades of blue plus pinks and whites,
their leaves broader, glossier.

They will sway more rhythmically
at the hint of a breeze, and toss their heads.
At the drum of a woodpecker, listen: one of them
will start to stamp.

They won't eat till nearly midnight
and then will go clubbing till four, long after their English cousins
are in bed.

When not dancing they will win Wimbledon,
build high speed trains and fantastic cathedrals.
They will save their broken plates to make mosaics.

On warm summer nights they will stroll
en familia through the parks and tree-lined squares,
the young talking phones and mopeds.
They will be in two minds about animal rights.
The grandmothers will remember Franco.

The men will sit in bars eating octopus, discussing
Gareth Bale.

Their tearaways will get roadside shrines.

Complete strangers – bluebells you hardly know –
will say *hola* to you.

First earlies

Sometimes, digging, a fleck of glaze
bright as a postage stamp winks up from its cast
and you, benign god, lift it
from how many centuries
to fragmentary afterlife.

No true god, though, you cannot project
its curve to cup or plate,
grow its flowers, restore its entity.
Whose food it bore, whose lips it touched –
what tunes they hummed,
which wars and despots ruled their lives –
are in that ditched letter.

Each of the vessel's unfound parts
and their scattered kin – tea-set
or dinner service – churn
in slow soil currents
further and further from home,
blind constellations

deep in soil's space – clay
that once wheeled through air, a butterfly –
turning, if earth spins long enough, to clay again.

IT HAS RAINED

Code

Dovebber, Jaduary ad Barch
the datiodal afflictiod bakes its rouds.
Wad grib afterdood you sedse
a cledched fist roud your epiglottis.
Baligd greblid, it hags id there
squeezig ad squeezig. Or baybe
you swallowed a dailbrush?

Do, you thindk, *do* – bore
like Hober Sibsod by the biddit.
I cad still breathe. You turd
the heatig up to baxibub, buscles achig
udtil dext bordig you fide
you've betaborphosed
idto a woolly babboth –

eyes streabig, dose ruddig,
gradba recobbeddig vitabid C
or baduka huddy. *Feed a code,* she dags
but you cad odely taste Barbite
ad TCP – there's a cebedt bixer
codvedtiod id your siduses
ad dow your ears have god fuddy,

rushig ad gurglig like a Badhattad
sewer. Your braid turded to bush
you draba queed it, sdortig ad sdeezig
od the screed which idforbs you
you are cobbod. You have
dasopharydgitis, rhidopharydgitis,
acute coryza or a code:

ad idfectiod which affects pribarily
the dose… the bost frequedt disease
id hubads, the average adult codtracts
two to three addually. *These idfectiods
have beed with hubadity sidce adtiquity.*
There is do cure. You are biserable
as sid. You are hubad.

Viral

Huddersfield, mid-September, and
the Grim Reaper is in Wilkinsons.
Six-foot-ten and almost behind me
I clock the black coat, hoodie
and scythe from the corner of my eye.
Not that he's not on every street
these days, but as I rarely see people
I know, I go back to his front,
meet his sockets and smile.
He grins.

A girl on the tannoy says I can easily
take out a parent-student card, pay money
straight in and my student can find
all they need for the new term here.
Where there's a Wilko, she chimes,
there's a way. But my student days
and my parents and child-bearing days
are gone so she's wrong, there's no way.

An image of the image if he struck,
scythe raised above the dust, pursues me
up the aisle. I'm after Strepsils and a saw.
Don't ask what he's here for.

Boar Lane, Leeds (1881)

John Atkinson Grimshaw

In those days shop windows meant business – just look
at the stonker for Taylors the Tailors: the Old Curiosity Shop
on steroids or laudanum certainly. Even the upper floor panes
seem inflamed with assistants' ambitions, the friction of string,
motion of adding machines – and thank heavens it's siling it down
again: Boar Lane glitters like Blea Tarn or Scarborough.
Nobody's looking out over the roofs to an age
where the smoke and the glory and half the young men disappear
or beyond that, to one where the shops themselves shrivel
to matterless thoroughfares, paperless offices, weightless cash –
so let's button our greatcoats, galoshes and gloves, shake off
the kerchinging of cast-iron tills and step with John Grimshaw
and his century into a river you can't step into twice.

Doubt

I used to think clouds crossed the sky
like ships – clods or balls of litter
winds might fray but mostly kicked
skyline to skyline, sunshine in the gaps assured
unless more snuck up over the horizon
while my back was turned. Until I grasped
that some must form in full view: condense
from empty-seeming blue in front of you.

Who sees this, though? Sixty-two years
waiting for rain to swell a crop or sun to dry
have yet to prove the science I accept:
matter born of vacancy – no clear trajectory,
just altered states: sheep, armadas, ice caps
radiant and lost before our faithless eyes.

Syzygy

Seen from the moon, the earth is jewel-bright:
a swirl of blues and yellows, greens and whites.
Surveying space in search of life, you'd know
immediately – it looks alive. You'd slow
your engines to a whisper and just stare.
Whole oceans shine: they really are azure;
the forests emerald; the deserts gold.
Even the clouds cling like wisps of packaging
around some infinitely precious thing
plucked from a ruin and unwrapped intact.
By contrast our old friend the moon looks whacked –
like some pasty impresario, glimpsed
through a midnight window, pulling strings
to keep the whole goddam show on the road.

Aloft

Nosing up above the joists I find
the long-lost or never had, here all along.

A space hopper, primed and perky
skims the glassfibre lagging

like an orange moon. Supine beside it,
a pogo stick. Grandmother's brown velvet cape
hand-sewn in London. One blue stocking.

Perranporth beach – the whole of it – the cottage
we'd have lived in if we'd moved there,

a crate of fizzy lemonade from the Pop Man.
I tuck two bottles under my arm

and, one-handed on the hopper, bounce
down the ladder, riding high.

Wwooom

Daddy goes out of the room
leaving me and the paper.
There are words I can read there.
And in the street. And in the shops.
There are words everywhere.

That black writing says Daily Mail.
Sometimes when I ask *is Popeye on*
Daddy looks in the paper and says no.
But sometimes he says no without looking.
I want to make him say yes.

I have read the whole of Andy Pandy.
But Popeye is funny. He eats spinach
and it goes into his arms and makes him strong.

The big pages rustle. I open each one
like a door. That says TV
and yes here it is: Pop
from Pop goes the Weasel and eye
two eyes and a Y. 4:00 – must be o'clock.

I fold the paper
and when Daddy comes back
I say *is Popeye on* and I feel hot
as he finds the same page
and when he says yes I say *Oh!*

I don't tell him what I did.
But when the television goes *wwooom*
and lights up and fizzes, it's like
a tin of spinach in my head.

'Hope'

G. F. Watts

The room
was dark even
with the light on.
The wallpaper was
brown. The bed was a
mountain you had to climb
onto. Half way down was a stone
hot water bottle. Auntie had been old
before you were born. There was an alcove
covered with a curtain. There was a picture
hanging from a cord, of a woman carrying
her own head. Behind it the wallpaper
was thick mould. A pigeon on the roof
sang *sorry, sorry*. The searchlight
sweeping the ceiling was a car.
Under the bed was big
enough for a body.
There was no
body. There
was nobody.

1970

The
first time
I had a shower
was in Paris. No one
I knew had one at home
or if they did they hadn't let on
but I knew the French had showers
and continental quilts. It was at the Centre
d'Accueil des Jeunes et de la Jeunesse which I
practised saying and I noticed there were loads of
showers and they were free so because I was fourteen
I didn't ask but just said I was going to have one. I checked
the coast was clear, took off all my clothes, turned it on and stood
in it for ages because that was what you did. I considered the sensation.
First it felt like being out naked in the rain and then like one of those dreams
where you forget your clothes. I reported some of this at breakfast to my parents
and brother who had used the sink. The Eiffel Tower and the Louvre were quite good too.

1973

That was the summer I worked in Kendals
Electricals when city department stores
stocked everything – tellies, washing machines
the lot – which young lads humped around
watched by girls from Records and Audio,

where I remember moaning to one called Stella
that I had to read all of Shakespeare
and she said *should be fun I love him* and I feared
for my intellect, thinking I'd done well
preferring Leonard Cohen to the Chi-lites,

and later in the canteen that boy
with the long straight hair and wide-mouthed smile
chatted me up so blatantly, and yes I said yes
and we kissed on Deansgate one of those
full-on clinches passers-by had to swerve round,

and all that June and July in his juddery Ford
we became connoisseurs of Mancunian dusks
till he played me off and I played it cool
as if it had been a rehearsal for the real thing
which would come soon surely,

though what I then wanted more than virginity
was my School Prize book token for French
which I left in his glove compartment and probably got spent
on Alex Comfort
or a text book on town planning.

Every June 10th

the only birthday card Dad ever gave you appeared
in its dog-eared envelope on the bureau, more or less
on cue. Embossed with a bunch of blowsy roses,
it must have cost something and been quite special
in 1952, but had yellowed and borne grey fingermarks
for as long as I could remember. *To my Wonderful Wife*
read the printed text, with *All my love, Derick*
beneath in blue-black Quink.

                                  Which clearly he meant,
for he never bought another. I guess it served
as a Valentine as well. And when urged
not to buy Mother's or Father's Day cards either –
that we should appreciate parents every day –
my brother and I dutifully saved our cash. Only now
can I see the gaps on the windowsill: gaps
no stack of rosy cards to a hospice could ever fill.

Pavane

Long after they were both gone,
after she was grown and had her own child – a son –
long after she had jettisoned more years
than she remembered,

she told me she had kept one thing
that summed up all the hopes they must have had
of her – and she, if only for some fond afternoon,
had of herself – dangled

pale, soft and supple on a pink satin ribbon,
the hope held out for girls: that with nothing
but their bodies, patience and enduring hunger
they can trade gravity

for grace – can pirouette,
arabesque and fouetté (each brutal move
dressed prettily in French) their way
to glory – to a world at their feet.

She kept not even two, but a single
ballet shoe. Fond. With all its freight
of foolish.

Unseen

The bench whose back and half-imagined view
we've climbed towards we find is occupied,
its length covered by a wreath which reads –
upside-down to us (and something stops us
stepping between it and the sea of fields
below, all June golds and greens: the houses,
quarries, silos, walls and fences, skeins of water,
stands of trees and gusts that make us feel
we cannot breathe enough) – MUMMY WHY.
The once-white roses, now tea-coloured, pose
the question every child asks first and every adult
needs, or takes, a life to answer. Right way up
it ricochets across north Staffordshire and then the sky
as if the miles might find an answer, or the answerer.

It has rained

and the blackberries you thought you'd miss
have sucked up the soaked earth to party one more week
around the snickets, building sites and lay-bys.
Behind allotment borders they cavort in parody
of garden soft fruits – shoot through cracks, prise walls apart
and manufacture vitamin-grenades free for the plucking.
Shouldn't such luck be suspect? If not poisonous, then
licensed? Yet there's enough for every thief and then some

always just beyond reach, tempting you to fall headlong
into that ditch-trickery. Hand over fist their promise loops
and spools, tangles and lures you down September lanes,
away from the learning world to where the untutored hedge
sets out its stall: its blood from stones, its wine
from rainwater, its alchemy.

Elizabeth I at fourteen

Today a month's rain lifted and she rode
to hounds at last. Bleeding now behind the arras
she counts down the ladies' slippered feet until
they're still, then conjugates *amer, amēris, amētur…*
the rhythms soothing as a papist's beads, wondering
if she will ever love – and of whom, to whom
as a princess she may speak, in truth, nothing forbidden her
but everything. She hears her heart. How like a beast's,
she wonders, are these innards, and how like a king's?
Beheadings she has seen, though not her mother's.
Spillage. Grallochings. If she must bleed let it be
no sword wound but God's. Rigid she lies
in the snuffered dark, fast as a swaddled child,
tempering her torso like a breastplate,
filling her quartered self with stones.

Ball game

My mistress' eyes are nothing like the sun.
Are anyone's, unless they've only one?
The human eye is multi-faceted –
an interplay of iris, lash and lid.
That eye without a pupil would be weird,
a dark spot on the sun, equally feared.
A yellow orb at dawn's a benediction,
a yellow eye the stuff of science fiction.
A pair of sparkling eyes can be alluring,
a pair of suns a bit less reassuring.
A lover may return your gaze in kind;
make doe-eyes at the sun and you'll go blind.
The sun's a nifty dancer with the moon,
but arguably love still calls the tune.

CLOZE PROCEDURE

Hinterland

Behind our eyes sometimes,
the lives we lead in dreams
we scarcely know we've had

which leave the mind rinsed,
the heart wrung, their imprint
like a watermark unnoticed

until held up to a light
that leaves us altered, older,
like the hollow space
the dead, the dear ones leave.

Behind our days, our nights,
behind our sparrow's flight
the ages unlived and to come,

the hand intangible, the land
we do not know we're from.

Inshallah

If any man comes to me without hating his father, mother, wife, children, brothers and sisters, yes and his own life too, he cannot be my disciple.
Luke 14:25

Wake, from sleepless summer heat. Make out dim corners
of the room. Things you never saw before. That box,
up on the wardrobe. Can't read the name. Stuff she doesn't tell you.
Dawn, filling the window square. Those patterned curtains
still not fixed. Said you'd get more hooks.

Reach carefully to cancel the alarm, an hour in hand.
Some car starting. Who, round here? Headlights scan
the walls. Quiet. The baby, breathing. Her age or a bit older
you used to dream of walking on the ceiling. Less clutter.
Thought everything would be that easy.

Bare feet on this new flooring, sound like sellotape.
Carpet to the bathroom softer. Sit to pee – quieter –
shit later. Maybe. Lose more minutes, gazing
at the crowded sill. Colgate. Angelina Ballerina. Don't flush.
Dodge the mirror. Face in half light not so clever.

How noisy houses are. Beds, cupboards, taps.
Clean chuds – respect yourself. Creep downstairs. No, give up
creeping in your own home. Orange juice. Fridge shudders.
Never a morning person. Dark t-shirt, good jeans, NY cap.
Not smart, not scruffy. Hardest line to tread.

That jacket. Money, phones. Car keys. Yale? In case.
Lift latch, too loud again. Pause split seconds on the step, then
close it, making sure it clicks. *Forsaking everything.*
You are responsible. It's time. You could be any man
just setting off to work.

News at ten

Huge on the step they stand, huger
in the kitchen. The ceiling lowers.
Walls close in. A walkie-talkie sputters
on the draining board. Their black bulk
crackles with the night city
like a door left open.

Sit down, someone says.
Chairs disappear. Helmets tilt
on worn pink formica. The room is wrong:
its lights too dim, its furniture too tired.

We are not ready
for their hard lines.

Literally

after Andrew Waterhouse

4 p.m., December dark. Forced out of Peace Studies
by the alarm I thread linoed corridors, concrete stairs
and a managers' mirrored lift to the Hi-vis Jacketed One
in the yard. She dandles a clipboard. I stare
at her hands – the bitten quick.

You just never know.
                        Nowhere's safe these days.

Standing under the moon, I admire its brutalism.
Clouds stride north. The screens inside
are tills. Icons rearrange themselves.

Money talks, though, doesn't it.
                        I mean, literally.

Shirts flap. Change jinks.

We are all numbers now.
                        Everyone wants to be famous.

I lean on the wall, swallowing rain.
Minutes pass.

That's it, more or less.
                        The way back in is the way out.

Cloze procedure

Complete using the words 'he', 'she', 'never':

He   taught her there, or anywhere else.
     caught her eye.
     chose his clothes carefully.
     wore his tightest jeans.
         She   wore her shortest skirt.

He   set up the after-school club with her in mind.
     asked her to stay back.
  was   alone with her.
        She   crossed her legs that way.

He   gave her a lift.
     stopped in a lay-by and kept the engine running.
Thought *others do. If I don't someone else.*

                cried.
He   wanted to protect her.

The family   tracked him down.
Two uncles   waited in the car park.   bled.
He   got headaches.
     married a nurse within the year.

     changed jobs. Hid in photos. Welcomed hair loss.
     woke in a sweat. Googled deed poll.
     lost his computer. Feared the phone, a knock. Sirens.

I would like to FORGET

the click of the door
the turn of the key
the swivel chair
the bed the grip the stink
the caravan sink
the leer from newspapers
and tv screens
the gagging shut up
wash your mouth out
sleepless nights the thought
I'd have to pay
when anyone was kind
the smell of you
on every man
the stomach-churning
phone calls letters
hospitals the fear
of being touched
the wondering if others
that it must have been
my fault somehow
the world a dirty joke
on kids especially girls
like me the big men
calling time too late
and keeping this a secret
so long I am still afraid
things will not change

Please can you fix this for me

Verdict

for being a kid
for not shutting up
for crying out loud
for crying

for sucking your thumb
for biting your nails
for chewing the sheet
for shaking

for wrecking the place
for taking up space
for wetting the bed
for whingeing

for making a noise
for getting a bruise
for banging your head
for bleeding

for burning yourself
for breaking an arm
for not being tough
for costing us
for crying
for crying out loud

Picasso's child

is dead, its head
cradled like an egg
its drawn features
fading already
in its mother's massive hand.
Thrusting her burden at us
she screams
into the susurrating gallery
whose backs are turned
staring at *Guernica*.

'Madre con niño muerto', Museo Reina Sofía, Madrid

Transit

The walls have folded themselves
in awkward places the floorboards
answer your step in different voices
choked with pieces of strangers' lives.
There's a room above where before
there was none and none below
where before there was one. The bed
must settle into this foreign space
as you shift in its sheets which already
smell alien. The road has crossed
to the other side the back door moved
to the front and the sun has gone
the wrong way round to morning.

Bradford

after Jamie McKendrick

Bradford the milly, the chilly, the everywhere hilly,
the Yorkshire, the canny, the Rajasthani,
the Polish, the Irish, the Romany,
the homeless, the homesick, the Manningham native,
the dislocated and the keypad-gated.

Bradford the hyped, the skyped, the lifetime saved-for,
the quixotic, the Quaker, the fortune-maker.
The fresh start, the loan shark, the business start-up,
the kohl-eyed, the streetwise, the Bollywood star-struck.

Bradford the Dissenter, the Luddite, the Chartist,
the in-your-face playwright, the bigger-splash artist.
The faith-schooled, grammar-schooled, scholarship-winning
part-time Philistine *can't be arsed innit.*

Bradford the once proud, wool-endowed, bloodied
but unbowed, Gothic, Italianate, Art-Deco run down.
The grandiose scrubbed-up municipal pompous.
The mansion, the prefab, the tentacled campus.

The bought-to-let, muddy-becked, moor-bound
and moribund. The vigilant vengeful, the honour-enslaved.
The Red Bull can on an Undercliffe grave.
The nest-studded trees in the central reservation,
finch robin blackbird singing. Bradford the brave.

Turning sixty

Off out tonight, gonna get mortal.
Facebook

I have not trolled the streets of central anywhere
at 2am in search of another WKD, bare-legged
in a boob tube with a buttock-skimming skirt,
tatts to the winds, clutch bag clamped
under one waxed armpit. I have not sat suppliant
at the nail technician's nor learned to walk
in six-inch heels to feel the blisters weep
and shrug off back pain. I have not kicked
my mother's vest habit to fix hypothermia
with tequila slammers, not learned to smile
easily at randomers giving it this or even
to call them that, nor to collapse in the doorway
of Age Concern moaning *god I'm mortal
get me home will you someone anyone* have I?

Footnote

There's a shoe[1] at the side of the road.

---

[1] Pairless and peerless its prospects are parlous:
for it, it's the end of the road. Did the shoe fall
out of a boot, the foot fall out of the shoe
or – over some footling issue – out with it, too?
Cast aside on its side, sidelined and footless,
was only the right shoe right for the left to be left
bereft, or was the right one also wrong?
Where are you, wearer? Shoe-shopping slipshod
from shop to shop for a leftover pair that's right?
Odds-on the wrong-footed right one lies in a lay-by
elsewhere, hoping a monopod hops by.

Then sometimes you'll think

of greenhouses – which are not green but transparent, named
not for themselves
but for a quality they might engender: their panes flyblown,
crusty – frames crying out
for a lick of something tender, like the care their charges get.

And you may think of the word dicotyledons for seedlings' two
first leaves –
those small arms waving *look, world, we are here* – forgetting too
soon
the disintegrating glass womb that they still need.

And you may think of greenhouses' secret armpit smell and
damp peaty hug,
surprised how something so weak-looking can contain such
heat, comforting at first
then coaxing you to put down roots, mutate into some freak
vegetable;

and of their mess – the runtish tools. Yogurt pot archive.
Margarine museum.
Plastic bottles with 'harmful' crosses. Something blackish-
brown, in a jar. On the floor
a once-red watering can, now faded to old lady pink. The pink
of that geranium.

And you may think of how they all need attention. Think of old
ladies – their shared air
of resignation, life interrupted, things unsaid: trays and
eccentric crockery set out
as if somebody longed-for has turned up and then, as
unexpectedly, just left.

Case sensitive

Outgrown with dens and playclothes –
mantra of junior despots, drug squads
and spies – I have forgotten
the latest concoction

of eight or more unique, significant,
memorable, randomly-capital letters, numbers
and unpronounceable symbols

I must never write down or disclose
and which no one – even me – will associate
with me.

Care of the elderly

Lubricate movement every two years. Open the door in the trunk
below the face. Lift the pulley off the gut
and remove the weight. The top part, covering the movement
and the face, is called the hood.

Hands can be re-blued in one of three ways: using bluing fluid,
burying in sand and heating gently with a blowlamp,
or blackening in a candle flame then painting with clear lacquer.
If they have broken, mend with silver solder.

Having made sure there is no more dirt, old oil, damp or rust left,
carefully reassemble, putting the pendulum through the trunk door,
the gap in the seat board and the crutch. Do not try
to dismantle the movement spindle.

Wharfedale General

Poorhouse, workhouse, hospital – guise after guise –
females and males processed on opposite sides;
under the floor a lock-up for troublemakers.

Wind in the central archway shivers.
Concealed in the leaves of its carved Corinthian pillars
a vagina on one side, a penis on the other.

A mason's snigger, missed by Inspectors,
Guardians, city fathers? This was their entrance.
Inmates were brought to the back. Or

a warren of conduits, links and signs
for those in the know? A dark web, centuries old?

Jersey's *Haut de la Garenne* means 'top of the warren':
well-stocked hunting grounds, reserved for the king.

Deeper and darker the pit, when spade hits bone.
Deeper and darker the silence, closer to home.

'Are you sure you want to – ?'

Turn off the router, the route of confusion,
turn off – at the wall – the oven and digibox
harrying me with their time. Disempower
the handset, the tablet, the fitbit: stop
all these scammers and spammers,
texters and twitterers, phishers
and compliment-fishers dead.
This swarm of electrons
infesting our homes, zapping
brickwork and stone, fretting
skin down to bone – this Babel
of babblers' mishmash of messages –
get them out of my hair. Reclaim instead
the domains of the mind: stand
on its headlands, read its skies, breathe
its untrafficked air. Yes, I am sure.

Seeking inspiration

you're crawling along at 8.06 a.m.
when out of the corner of your eye
you see a man on top of the steeple
of St Andrew's, Oakenshaw. A live man,
standing on the pinnacle
as if he owned the place, surveying
the packed aisle of the M606:
a boiler-suited messiah
breaking his journey one way or other
in a small, providential crow's nest
of scaffolding, contemplating
a Monday morning rush-hour miracle.

In deep

Overnight it hooded us, that first fall. How could we have known
it wouldn't stop? Against the sound of spinning tyres
and snowploughs giving up, we shovelled till our fingers froze,
our arms and backs gave out and we were cut off
by the mountains made. Something about this, though, we
    would not buy.
That what they'd warned us of was happening? That it was too
    late now
to eat or try to sleep above the revving motors and the wind?
One by one each engine died.

Dusk after dusk, dawn after dawn, those angel feathers bore down
on us. Three days and the roads were gone, studded only by the
    tumuli
of cars and trucks, their drivers trapped or dazed, clutching
    phones and keys
to homes they wouldn't see again. Blizzards erased tracks, shrank
    walls
to tracery and whipped up gaunt topographies. Sheep huddled
    by their bales,
those ochre clumps like embers. Over weeks of dark days and
    pale nights,
farmers combed the wild terrain, grieving, fathoming the cost.

Dismissing forecasters who saw no end in sight, we paced
by windows trying to take it in, or glued ourselves to screens
jittery with tall tales: of burst pipes forming petrifying waterfalls,
planes grounded, ambulances lost, turbines buried, power off
    and on
then off. London sunk, the Seine skied along,
Liberty up to her ears, her torch icicles. Then
nothing. The server – servers – down.

Next day dawned darker – windows covered like the eyelids of a
  corpse.
We put on all our clothes and climbed shakily to skylights.
  Pushed.
We knew then that our lives were places we would not return to.
The old, the sick collectively forgotten, we hauled furniture
  upstairs
and burnt it, cleaned out freezers to make warmer beds. The
  young set off
directionless for lawless towns. Years later one who came back
told us what we'd guessed. Greenland was a green land,

Europe, North America and China the skewed tundra, begging
from mild Africa; the cool subcontinent. The old poles we re-
  imagined
toppled off their footings like deposed dictators. Most of what
  we owned
we buried with our former selves, redundant in this new
  economy
of grit and drudgery – machines a joke, the wheel history.
Thirty years, it must be – without seasons you lose track,
miss certainties. A leaf's waxy circuitry. The solar power of trees.
  Earth
as we knew it. Spiders. Blue sky. Stars. We never said goodbye.

After Rothko

Black on grey, 1969

This is not the night sky, teeming with more than we know.
This is not the abyss. Not a black hole. Not unremitting black.
This is not a compulsion to make something out of nothing.
This is not nihilism, nor existentialism. This is not the choice.
This is not our future, not our past, not the next step. This is
not the frontier of human understanding. This is not infinity.
This is not the dawn of creation, nor its end. This is not the
consequence of vaunting ambition. This is not an astronaut's
vision nor a transfixed audience's nightly television. This is not
the science of proportion. This is not the state of this world as
we leave it for others. This is not tragic. This is not the edge.
This is not a slight curvature. This
is not the shape of every planet in
existence. This is not featureless grey.
Not a moonscape. Not scorched earth.
Not ruined Manhattan. Not a runway.
Not a victim's last view. Not cold war.
Not depression. Not the colour of
thought. It is paint on paper. It is just

Acknowledgements

Thanks are due to editors/judges of the following, who first published some of these poems: *Agenda* 52, *www.antiphon.org.uk* 2017; *Beehive Poets* 2014, 2015; *Bridport Prize Anthology* 2015; *Brittle Star* 28; *The Troubadour Poetry Prize* 2015; *Grey Hen Press* 2014; *www.leadstoleeds.com*; *Lightship International Competition Anthology* 2012; *www.liveencounters.net* 2018; *www.londongrip.org* 2017; *Magma* 66; *Obsessed with Pipework* 55; *Orbis* 147; *Pennine Platform* 81; *Poetry Monthly* 118; *Poetry Salzburg Review* 31; *Red Shed Poetry Competition/Currock Press* 2017; *Riptide* 2013 Vol. 9; *Stand* 215; *The Frogmore Papers* 89; *The High Window* 56, 2017; *The North* 52; *The Rialto* 60; *www.yorkmix.net* 2015.

Special thanks are due to Nicholas Bielby of Graft Poetry, who published my full-length collections *Without a Dog* (2008) and *Eleven Wonders* (2012); to The Poetry Business for their Pamphlet Prize (*The Half-Mile-High Club*, 2007); and to Peter Sansom for his original encouragement.

'Inshallah' came fourth in the Raise Your Banners Political Poetry Competition 2009. 'Then sometimes you'll think' won the Lightship International Poetry Competition 2012. 'How can I tell if the bluebells in my garden are Spanish?' came third in the Bridport International Poetry Competition 2015.